LOOKING AT ART (WITH YOUR EYES CLOSED)

This book is about the power of art.

The room, the art gallery, only has four walls but it can expand, through your perceptions, to contain much more.

Perhaps it can be everything?

My volume confers value on you, the viewer, as the potential artist. It makes you, for the moment of looking, the centre of things. It encourages you to trust your own intuition.

Step into a new version of reality.

In my own history, the gallery has been an important place, an area of discovery, of experiment. When I couldn't access these ideas in real life, the exhibition space gave me the opportunity to take a chance, to play. And so allowed me to explore the boundaries of myself – through visual image, philosophy, new experiences, shock.

I became the artist by being there.

Therefore, I offer this book to you with a full heart, knowing the impact that art has had on me. I trust that it can have the sar

Look, see, feel.

LOOKING AT ART (WITH YOUR EYES CLOSED)

Michael Atavar's creative courses from Tate: experiments in everyday seeing

Kiosk
PUBLISHING

info@look-at-art.com
www.look-at-art.com

ISBN 978-0-9531073-5-3

A catalogue record for this book is available from the British Library.

Artwork by Richard Scarborough. Typeset in Trade Gothic.

Ars earum rerum est quae non sciuntur

ART?
IT'S ALL
ABOUT
YOU.

CONTENTS

INTRODUCTION

This book is inspired by my courses at Tate – 'Creative Process' (2014), 'The Creative Act' (2015) (at Tate Modern) and 'Experimental Making (Creating From Everyday)' (2016) (at Tate Britain), delivered as part of Tate's Public Programme.

In the final session of 'The Creative Act', one of the participants said in front of the class, 'After following the course, I now understand that it's what I feel about the art that counts, not the work itself.'

I suddenly realised that what I had been teaching at Tate was not a series of classes about art practice but a course in self-actualisation; whilst I had always been interested in this area, it took this piece of feedback for me to understand that it had been my real, underlying purpose.

It's the 'I' that counts.

I took the comments as my cue to write a book about the subject. The volume was written quite quickly and I tried not to edit my words too much – I wanted to convey my sense of excitement at this discovery and transmit it to the reader.

'Looking At Art (With Your Eyes Closed)' positions you, the viewer, not the artist, as the centre of the creative process. I realise that this turnaround is not easy to activate.

Try it – with application it can be achieved.

Follow the 52 sections in the book and step through this journey, simply using your self as the guide. With some patience and trust you can place your identity at the centre of the gallery experience.

A further note: one way of reading this volume is to carry the book with you when you visit the exhibition. If you get stuck, open the pages at random and follow the instructions that you find there. Explore the space in this unpredictable way, travelling down less familiar routes.

Everything can be discovered in the gallery (it's a place where you can reveal a lot about yourself).

Follow this book as a guide and, step by step, unpack the experiences that you find there.

You are the artist.

Michael Atavar

FOREWORD

Tate Public Programmes develop inspiring and engaging public events that create platforms for conversations with audiences about art and society.

Through collaboration between artists, educators and other participants, Tate and its collection have the potential to be opened up by a diverse range of activities and experiences in the galleries, online and beyond.

Audiences join in an exchange of ideas explored by art and artists, reflecting upon the relevance of art to our own lives.

Learning about the ways in which artists work helps us to understand how we too might consider ourselves and the world around us differently.

The courses with Michael at Tate are a perfect example of this.

Over a number of weeks, participants engage with the ideas and processes of artists and each other, extending their conversations beyond the works of art on display.

This isn't easy. The galleries at Tate aren't a place to sit back and let others do the hard work for you. But for those prepared to invest in themselves and challenge the ways in which they do things every day, Michael offers the opportunity to reach new levels of understanding about their own ability, questioning yet encouraging them along the journey.

And more often than not, those who share this experience together form strong bonds, creating their own kind of community.

I very much enjoyed working with Michael and through his courses have often found myself questioning my own relationship to art, the people in the gallery and those outside it.

I look forward to exploring these exercises in many other museums and galleries.

Joseph Kendra

Joseph Kendra has programmed talks, courses and workshops at Tate, The Photographers' Gallery, The National Gallery and elsewhere.

LOOKING AT ART (WITH YOUR EYES CLOSED)

Michael Atavar's creative courses from Tate: experiments in everyday seeing

WHAT'S THE FEELING?

You are in the gallery and the work is in front of you.

How do you proceed?

At this moment it's worth remembering that it's the feeling that the piece evokes in you that's important.

Nothing else matters.

Of course, there is content, form, colour – but put that aside just now. What does the painting or sculpture provoke in you?

Don't confuse a thought for a feeling; don't allow an intellectual process to take the place of an emotion.

If you start with –

- The artist intends
- Historically
- A formal conceit
- Their colour palette

then you are on the wrong track.

Instead, start with 'I'.

'I feel', 'I understand', 'I believe'.

Make yourself the subject.

The artwork is merely a vehicle to get you to the best version of yourself.

MAKE YOURSELF THE SUBJECT.

IT'S THE TOTALITY OF THE EXPERIENCE THAT COUNTS

When you are in the gallery, don't forget what's around you.

I find that the artwork in front of me is only a part of the experience of seeing art, a totality that I don't discount.

So, for example, if –

- The space is noisy.
- You are alone.
- There is a school party.
- The view to the work is blocked.
- You can't concentrate.

All these factors are a part of your reading of the situation.

Remember, it's what you bring to the artwork that counts, not what the artwork brings to you.

This might be the opposite of what you have previously been taught: the primacy of the artist, the value of culture, the integrity of the experience.

(Turn it upside down.)

I'd like you to consider a more performative approach – where everything that comes into your eyes and ears as you look at the work is also the work.

Everything that you see is important.

IT'S WHAT YOU BRING TO THE ARTWORK THAT COUNTS.

TRUST YOUR FIRST IMPRESSIONS

You have come to the gallery with the best of intentions; however, if you don't like the work in front of you, it's OK to move on.

Trust your first impressions and try not to undermine them. These feelings might be: I am happy, I feel sad, I am enlivened, I feel scared.

Always use the 'I' word to frame your thoughts.

Often when I arrive at an exhibition, I move rapidly through the space, trusting what I see there. Then, once I get to the end, I move backwards through the gallery, focusing on the things that held my attention the first time round.

There is value in staying and value in moving on.

My attitude is: the gallery is there to give me something, not the other way around – I must provide something, some expertise to the exhibition.

Often we regard every cultural institution as inviolable.

It's not true.

What you see with your own eyes and hear with your ears is your reality. In the course of your research you might take on further knowledge that could alter your perspective.

(Keep open.)

ALWAYS USE THE 'I' WORD TO FRAME YOUR THOUGHTS.

BE PRETENTIOUS

When you look at the work of art, involve all your perceptions, even if these thoughts don't always add up.

Often we arrive at the gallery doubting our own ideas.

We question what we notice, we read the catalogue – all perhaps to stop ourselves from having a direct relationship with what's in front of us.

Just look.

Let the image sink into you.

What are your feelings?

If they are a jumble, don't worry. Thoughts are often like that. Be pretentious. If you like the blue, say 'I like the blue'. You can even use the word 'aquamarine', if you want to.

We are experiencing heightened emotions all the time – from our eyes, our body, our brain, our fingertips. Most of the time, due to social etiquette, we tend to blank these out.

The sports event and the gallery are two of the opportunities left open to us. Here we can, at least, experiment with these qualities.

Don't worry about what everyone else is doing – go on your own journey, at your own pace.

Being pretentious is a way of testing your own limits.

GO ON YOUR OWN JOURNEY, AT YOUR OWN PACE.

SPEND 30 MINUTES IN EACH ROOM

Spend a minimum of 30 minutes in each room, or 30 minutes with each painting.

Some ideas only emerge over time – so engage fully with the piece.

Involve all your senses.

Stay with it.

It's often only at the end of a process, when you are bored and weary, that your defences will drop and you will be able to see something for the first time: a theme, an image, a feeling.

Most people will spend less than 30 seconds in front of each work of art. Click. They will record it on their camera and then move on.

Be aware of this attitude when you look. Attempt to do the opposite. Engage in deep looking. Try not to pass by too quickly.

Be mindful that when you move on too rapidly, you avoid something difficult. Difficulty is the lens through which you will finally see something new.

Often when I spend this amount of time in the gallery, I sit on the floor and look at the passersby, grounding myself in my own deep watching.

I see the sculptures, a fly buzzing, the people, the light.

DIFFICULTY IS THE LENS THROUGH WHICH YOU WILL FINALLY SEE SOMETHING NEW.

SIT DOWN (IF NECESSARY ON THE FLOOR)

When you spend 30 minutes in front of an artwork, you can try different strategies for looking –

- Draw an artwork.
- Listen to other people.
- Write in your notepad.
- Focus on one item.

Sometimes you become a vehicle for just looking.

If you sit, rather than stand, you step out of the hurly-burly of the gallery procession, the click and move on, and become something different (part of the artwork?).

You stand outside and look in.

This allows you to have a different perspective.

Things arrive, at their own pace. Notions, thoughts. There is an enviable depth to the process – because you have committed to the act of looking.

Try it and see what happens.

You might notice that you become more visible. People will look at you. Try to take this in your stride and not worry too much about what other people think.

If the gallery is liberating, it's because of these things: it's an opportunity for you to try out different personal attitudes to life, without committing wholeheartedly to the practice of change.

(Art is a theatre.)

SPEND 30 MINUTES IN FRONT OF THE ARTWORK.

CLOSE YOUR EYES

This might appear a strange instruction when looking at visual material: to close your eyes. However, remember the first page of this book – it's about your feelings.

Your interiority forms the basis for your own looking, so turn inside to see what's out there.

Your version of reality is not what is real, it's based on your experience and background. So why not use that?

Stand directly in front of the work so that the piece occupies all your field of vision. Remain motionless, eyes closed. Stay there for a minimum of 5 minutes. Do not act on anything, but be alert to your interior process.

What do you really see?

Sense the image, without looking at it. Translate any images or colours that you find into feelings.

Do you feel –

- Sad?
- Uplifted?
- Embarrassed?
- Angry?
- Happy?
- Disappointed?
- Excited?
- Confused?

Are any of these feelings present in the work of art?

TRANSLATE ANY IMAGES OR COLOURS THAT YOU FIND INTO FEELINGS.

AS THINGS POP UP, WRITE THEM DOWN

This is a technique that I frequently use to sharpen my own perceptions of the art that is in front of me.

The Exercise

As you look at the work, write down your ideas in a notepad. I suggest that you choose cheap pens and paper (perhaps even the free sheet handout from the gallery). The purpose: to avoid anything becoming too precious, too grandiose.

If you are using a crumpled-up sheet of paper, you won't feel too bad about making errors, or putting a line through a sentence. However, if you have invested in an expensive line of stationery, you might be more circumspect.

Write down your immediate responses as they occur, making little effort to be concise or grammatical. Try not to frame your thoughts as complete sentences but scribble the results, as fast as they come.

- Feelings are pertinent.
- Adjectives are excellent.
- Lists are creative.
- Mistakes are valuable.

Errors are good; they express something that is pushing through, not yet placed in a context, unformed and free; something that might be useful to explore in your own appreciation of art.

WRITE DOWN YOUR IMMEDIATE RESPONSES AS THEY OCCUR.

USE YOUR OWN VOICE

Everything is available to you, to your creativity. It might not feel like that; however, it's the truth.

You are the prism through which the artwork comes alive. It's nothing without you. Even the classics, the greatest works of art, are just dusty relics without the contemporary glance from you, breathing new life into them.

A museum is just a receptacle for you to bring the past back into existence – through your breathing.

If, as I believe, the purpose of art is to evoke feelings, another way of activating these emotions, of taking ownership of the work, is to rename it according to your own rules.

- Choose a one-word title.
- Adopt something that is evocative.
- Name it with a string of adjectives.
- Put a colour in the heading.

Always using your own voice, your own attitudes, to inform the decision.

Even if you simply number the pieces in the gallery – 1, 2, 3, 4, 5 etc., you make a conscious choice to bring the artwork into a relationship with your own individuality.

Whatever you do, just do it as quickly and as robustly as you can manage.

YOU ARE THE PRISM THROUGH WHICH THE ARTWORK COMES ALIVE.

GIVE IT ANOTHER NAME

For example, if you see 'The Hay Wain', you might rename it as 'A Shallow River, a Watchful Dog and a Muddy Cloud'.

This act of iconoclasm turns the subject upside down and brings it into a relationship with you –

- What part of you is shallow?
- Are you watching, or paying attention?
- Is the cloud really muddy?

Do you just brush this piece off as an 'old master' without really looking too deeply at it?

Probably.

This technique encourages you to make a real connection with what's in front of you, rather than moving on rapidly, confirming something clichéd about what you have just 'seen'.

(Usually we are not really looking at all; we are just confirming with our ego that everything is OK.)

I choose Constable as an example here, but you might try this exercise with 'Mona Lisa', 'Guernica', or 'Sunflowers'.

Build a personal, feeling connection to these artworks by the act of renaming.

Is this a radical act?

Why not?

BUILD A PERSONAL, FEELING CONNECTION TO THESE ARTWORKS BY THE ACT OF RENAMING.

WHAT IS UN-SAY-ABLE?

I often encourage people to take the opposite view, to turn it upside down, to say the un-say-able, in pursuit of a personal connection.

You don't degrade what is already there (the 'Mona Lisa' will always exist), you simply add your own perspective to a familiar formula.

However, through these methods, you can build a direct relationship to what you see.

This technique already has a rich history in art –

* Marcel Duchamp's mischievous moustache on Leonardo's masterpiece.
* Mark Wallinger's 'Where There's Muck', a deconstruction of Thomas Gainsborough's painting 'Mr and Mrs Andrews'.
* Joan Miro's use of cheap 70s reproductions to paint over in his trademark style.

I find this process liberating; turning what is revered into something new.

Look at what is in front of you and speak out loud what is un-say-able.

Remember, the artwork is the transitional object. It only serves you. It is not an independent entity, but an extension of your self.

You can say what you like.

TURN IT UPSIDE DOWN.

USE THE 'I' WORD

'I' is the magic word that turns what you see into 'you'.

Use it liberally in your estimation of what's in front of you.

- I see.
- I feel.
- I believe.
- I understand.

Sometimes I go right up to the piece and look at the surface, so that it becomes my sole area of vision and I examine the edge, the construction, the wear, the frame.

I go close so that my 'eye' becomes my 'I'.

The 'I' is a dense landscape, a rich terrain.

Often we are encouraged to abandon this 'I' in search of some objectivity, a sense of art history, a process of contextualisation.

I say drop that approach in the rubbish bin for a while and look at your innate responses, as if you were seeing it for the first time.

Use a physical technique and place yourself right in there, with the paint and the glue, the Plexiglas and the light.

What qualities do you have?

Are you as oily and as sticky as a brush stroke?

LOOK AT YOUR INNATE RESPONSES, AS IF YOU WERE SEEING IT FOR THE FIRST TIME.

LIQUIDITY

The difficulty of seeing art is the challenge of not being in one fixed position, of avoiding cultural and personal baggage – therefore remaining liquid to the proposition.

I see therefore I am (an inversion of René Descartes).

Solid, confirmed expectations, reduced, lacking curiosity are a form of defence: if you were able for a moment to abandon your fixed posture, you might learn something new.

But how to do that?

One tip that I have picked up from Gestalt Therapy is to physically act out any problem; through the body it's possible to transcend the mind's own obstacles and find a new solution.

So, be liquid.

Wave your arms like seaweed, slide backwards and forwards, do a turn around the space and approach the artwork obliquely, like a thief.

In this state of liquidity (the mind suppressed), what are your impressions?

'Criticism' is the hard surface of things, 'liquidity' presents a soft contact with objects: if you can't touch the work, then approach it with the body's echo.

Liquid day to day.

I SEE
THEREFORE
I AM.

DETUNE YOUR EYES

Another way of integrating this enviable liquidity is to detune your eyes.

The Exercise

Sit and half-close your eyes, as if you are on your way to sleep. In this state of semi-sentience, look at everything around you, as if it were one thing, not separated from you by your body, but swimming in the same soup.

Now approach the artwork with this same technique. Can everything that is in this room be regarded as one entity, one thing?

If the paintings or sculptures are the same, what is the thread that connects them? What's the first word that comes into your head to describe this feeling – a string of lights, a cord, an alignment, a pulse of connection?

Alternatively, is there a conflict? Can these works be propelled away from each other in a blast of disgust, disconnection and devaluation?

The DYE ('detune your eyes') method can be applied to most creative situations. Try the technique when you want to melt into your creativity. In this way you draw on C.G. Jung's creative unconscious to support your choices.

This is always useful.

You are not alone; people are there to help, even if this remains abstract, invisible.

CAN EVERYTHING THAT IS IN THIS ROOM BE REGARDED AS ONE ENTITY, ONE THING?

PUT YOURSELF IN THE FRAME

As William S. Burroughs says, don't look in, look out.

What I take from his statement is, don't dwell on what's inside, but look outside yourself onto the physical world and record 'what it is'.

Do this every day and you have a practice – it's really as simple as that.

When you look at the canvas, instead of struggling with its meaning, put yourself in it. Be the image. Use the magic 'I' word in order to fully inhabit its landscape.

Step inside.

- I am blues.
- I am patches.
- I am pillows.
- I am drips.
- I am diagonals.
- I am pale squares.
- I am shaded edges.
- I am yellow Lego bricks.

(John Hoyland's 'Advance Town 29.3.80'. The catalogue happens to be on my desk as I write this, so I use it as my primary material to illustrate the idea.)

Don't look at the colour, be it.

Don't step away, occupy the vastness.

With your mind's eye, be the canvas.

DON'T LOOK AT THE COLOUR, BE IT.

TAKE A STEP FORWARD

In order to fully occupy the experience of the object, take one step forward.

With this step, try to focus on moving ahead; not merely physically, but allow the possibility for something to shift.

Imagine an invisible line in front of you and step across it, into the next phase, the void, the impossible, the future.

(I am thinking of Yves Klein's 'Le Vide'.)

Try it and see.

If nothing happens, don't worry. Some things come with practice. Each time you are in the gallery, attempt the same thing, and over time observe the changes in you.

These might be subtle. Yet slowly the body finds its own centre, moving forward inexorably, progressively.

With each step say 'I am stepping into a new place'.

Recognise that this possibility is not exterior to you, but part of your interior world. You can alter the mood of the space; you have that ability within you.

The world of art is not just dead wood and inert plastic; it is not merely discarded newspaper or dirt accumulated on the carpet – it has an energy of change about it.

And all those changes come from within you.

IMAGINE AN INVISIBLE LINE IN FRONT OF YOU AND STEP ACROSS IT.

SLOW DOWN

The gallery space is a zone of its own.

I think of the art gallery as a time machine, not limited by conventional boundaries of form or space. It's more like a flare, shot on a trajectory into no-man's land.

To occupy this space completely, take off your watch, put your camera away, shut down your mobile phone, hide your credit card.

(Really, you don't need to purchase anything to have an experience.)

You can have a penniless epiphany.

Slow down.

Take an hour or two out of normal time and drift between the galleries, following your nose.

Many times my own heightened experiences of art have occurred when something serendipitous has happened: I came in out of the rain, I couldn't buy a ticket to the intended show, I took the lift to the wrong floor, I picked up a book in the cafeteria.

We expect the epiphany of art to be in front of something big that will overwhelm us.

Often I'm flipped on a coin; a fortuity pushes me towards the void where unexpectedly the clinks of magic flicker in the accidental.

Slow down and allow this to happen.

TAKE OFF YOUR WATCH, PUT YOUR CAMERA AWAY, SHUT DOWN YOUR MOBILE PHONE.

DRAW IT

One way of making a direct connection with what you are looking at is to record the image on paper, however sophisticated or primitive the results.

You might be put off by this suggestion. Yes, a drawing can be the most crudely effected caricature. It's not the point. The purpose is to merely give you a direct connection with what you see – a line that comes from the object, to your eye and hand, flowing directly to the pen.

Don't invest unnecessarily in materials and thereby place a barrier between you and the action. Choose cheap paper and a normal felt-tip. Don't give any space to your critical tendency by adding further layers of difficulty.

Select the first pen that comes to hand.

Additionally, it's often useful to use Alexander Calder's continuous line technique.

Try it this way –

The Exercise

Draw what you see, each time not lifting the pen from the paper.

Don't worry if you make mistakes, or if it's not what you expect.

Keep going.

DRAW WHAT YOU SEE, EACH TIME NOT LIFTING THE PEN FROM THE PAPER.

TURN IT UPSIDE DOWN

If you get stuck with your way of seeing, or if your drawing frustrates you, turn the piece of paper in your hand upside down.

What happens?

Sometimes this simple act can allow different feelings to come through, unhindered by your mind.

The ego is always protecting you, allowing no social embarrassment to take place; to put you in the right sector in the hierarchy. Turning things upside down inverts that process and forces you to look at them from another angle.

If you upend an image 180 degrees, you will highlight the unconscious part of yourself, so feelings that have previously remained hidden will suddenly be revealed.

Focus on the border, the fringes – when this happens, which shadowy elements become clear?

It's a magic trick of deep psychological impact; when you step into the potential of non-linear interpretation, you enter a profound space of self from which there is no going back.

Be careful. The upside down can transform you.

Try the process gradually, experimenting each time with what you can tolerate.

Flip it in stages, 10 degrees at a time.

FOCUS ON THE BORDER, THE FRINGES.

OR TURN YOURSELF UPSIDE DOWN

You can take this action one stage further by turning yourself upside down.

As you look at the artwork –

- Angle your head 90 degrees.
- Look backwards, turning right or left.
- Place you head between your legs.
- See the reverse in a mirror.

These intentional inversions will splinter the work, so that it is not seen through the usual filter of 'right' angle seeing.

In this place of new vision, you will integrate your perceptions into the work, making it as much about your feelings as the object itself.

Remember, it's not the purpose of the work to hold its own hermetic energy; it must be completed, seen, by you to give it an impact.

Or if it has a sealed difference, a closed-off element, it's this quality reflected in you that counts.

Accidentally, through this technique, you are integrating something quite radical, soaking up the historical energy from The Diggers, Proudhon, Gerard Winstanley and Kropotkin.

You are looking finally at the world turned upside down. What do you want? 'Right' angle seeing forever, or something different?

WHAT DO YOU WANT? 'RIGHT' ANGLE SEEING FOREVER, OR SOMETHING DIFFERENT?

MAKE A MAP

Another way of playing with this idea of the upside down is to make a map.

Try it this way –

The Exercise

Take your drawing of the object (or a copy of your original) and cut the paper up into numerous square pieces – six or ten is a good number.

Then sit on the floor and move your pieces around.

Often it's better to choose the separate elements by chance, reassembling them completely at random. This way you don't integrate your logical mind but allow something new to come through.

Finally, place the randomised elements back into a conventional grid and see what has happened.

Are there any configurations that give you a new perspective on the work?

Even if you have picked up, by accident, the reverse of your drawing, don't disallow these elements, but accept them as part of the whole.

The blanks scattered across your new canvas, or the pieces upside down, integrated into the frame, can give you a radically new meaning to the artwork.

Perhaps by suggesting what is blank, absent?

CHOOSE THE
SEPARATE
ELEMENTS
BY CHANCE,
REASSEMBLING
THEM
COMPLETELY
AT RANDOM.

CHANGE FIGURATIVE TO ABSTRACT

In one group that I was running at Tate, we followed the 'map exercise' from the previous page; in this instance we worked with a series of photocopied images of a classic painting, cut into quarters, placing the remodelled squares in different relationships to each other.

The configurations were –

- Only the sky squares of the painting showing.
- In a long line of steps, leading towards the giant windows.
- Scattered across the floor, deconstructed.

One participant turned over all the pieces, until they showed only the white reverse, and piled them up, making a rough, angled cross.

Thus, what was originally figurative became abstract.

For him the classic painting meant 'nothing'; it was void. Perhaps it was simply a homage to Kazimir Malevich?

Try this 'figurative to abstract technique' during your next visit to the gallery.

In your mind's eye, turn what is solid, figurative, into simple abstract shapes.

Make bodies float, change skies into stripes and blur the boundary between self and outside.

What does the colour say?

TURN WHAT IS SOLID, FIGURATIVE, INTO SIMPLE ABSTRACT SHAPES.

GET YOUR HANDS DIRTY

It's time for a short philosophical interlude: namely, get your hands dirty.

Art is not out there, beyond you, in a separate place, only reserved for those 'in the know'. It's full of possibilities for your personal growth.

Yet the only bridge that activates this potential is action.

You cannot step back and expect the art to come to you. Neither should you be the conduit for its self-completion, making the artist only a passive executor of your individual needs.

In fact, the middle way is ideal, where your thoughts and actions complete a circle, Gestalt-style.

Go to the gallery with your eyes and ears open, ready to access something new. Do not simply passively record art on your camera or mobile phone, one click, and move on, but spend some time attempting to understand what's in front of you, engaging in active seeing.

Active seeing is –

- Minimum 30 minutes.
- Draw the item.
- Write about your experience in your notepad.
- Note the totality of the gallery visit.
- Fold in all the realities of the room.

This list also acts as a summary of the book so far.

GO TO THE GALLERY WITH YOUR EYES AND EARS OPEN.

DON'T READ THE LABEL OR LISTEN TO THE GUIDE

One way of focusing on your own feelings is to ignore the labels next to the paintings.

If it's an important name, you might feel inclined to give it more credibility; if it's someone minor you could unconsciously offer less value. Instead, trust your own experience of the work: it's your feelings that count.

Remember that you are the conductor of your own journey through the space.

Also, for once, decline the gallery headset and inhabit the work silently, without a guide to help you. Switch off audio, and listen with your eyes. Art history is a great tool to help you contextualise the artwork, but use it sparingly, and not as a sticking plaster to avoid your own experience of the gallery.

Instead, follow your own instinct. So if you feel that you don't want to start in Room One (although the guide tells you it's a must), but think you should start instead in Room Fifteen, then just do it. Move rapidly there.

You make the space happen, you buy the ticket.

Make it a reflection of your own needs.

Often I dwell on very few elements and move rapidly through other rooms, in favour of what is important to me. It's a method that concentrates the attention on one or two things.

TRUST YOUR OWN EXPERIENCE OF THE WORK.

DON'T TAKE PHOTOGRAPHS

I don't want to write a list of 'don't dos'.

However, try not to take photographs of the artworks.

I was once in a large public gallery in Toulouse and as I was leaving I saw a man arrive at the show, walk into the room, automatically take a photograph of the first painting in the exhibition and immediately move on.

The shock of his approach was such that I've always remembered this attitude.

It was as if he didn't see the picture at all but was intent on capturing it, as one might stalk a lion in a big game reserve.

Art as capture.

When you are photographing you are not looking. It feels like you are seeing, framing the picture, recording through the lens, but you have already switched off. You have gone into collecting mode, adding to your document files.

If you want to record your own experience of the painting, try writing about it or drawing a quick sketch. Of course, these activities take you into a deeper kind of seeing and are therefore more difficult.

The quick snap of the camera is you shutting down to your own experience. Try a 'longer exposure'; sit in front of the same image for 30 minutes and see what emerges.

TRY A 'LONGER EXPOSURE'.

MAKE A LIST OF QUALITIES

One way of supporting your personal relationship with what's in front of you is to make a list of its qualities. Rather than identifying what is inviolable about the object, you are simply noting the shifting elements that make up the piece. Don't worry about what is 'right' – there is no right answer, merely what you observe.

Whatever you notice is the artwork.

Some qualities might be simple –

- Big.
- Wide.
- Tall.
- Narrow.

Others more complex –

- Relationship.
- History.
- Architecture.
- Meaning.

If you treat both as the same, you won't get bamboozled by complexity. Note down your impressions quickly in your notepad. This concretisation of feeling facts will help you, by solidifying them on the page.

Also, list-making can be a creative act. Take some pleasure in recording your responses and note the relationship between different items in your directory.

Treat the list as a small poem, a continuous text.

THERE IS NO RIGHT ANSWER, MERELY WHAT YOU OBSERVE.

CHOOSE SOMETHING THAT REPELS

Of course, those qualities that you identify don't need to be things that are attractive.

You might be drawn to beauty, intelligence, harmony, but that might not be what is in the work – perhaps there is dissonance, alarm, intimidation.

Often if you recoil from these elements, they are the ones that it's useful to focus on.

Stay with what repulses you.

In the gallery, if your tendency is to look for themes across several artworks, then do the reverse – isolate a canvas and concentrate solely on this one object.

I recently worked with a client at an exhibition of Gustav Metzger 'Towards Auto-destructive Art 1950–1962'. In this show we focused on the piece 'Recreation Of First Public Demonstration Of Auto-Destructive Art 1960', one of the more challenging works on display. However, when forced to explore the detail of this work, the viewer found sympathy, complexity, austerity – echoes of her own process. Normally, however, she would never have approached this work; difficulty provided its own reward.

Likewise, in one of my workshops where I asked people to bring their own images, it was a situation of contention – two conflicting pictures – that offered most fuel for the group's discussion.

(Clash of the 'Titians'.)

STAY WITH WHAT REPULSES YOU.

IMAGINE WHAT YOU ARE LOOKING AT DOESN'T EXIST

Paintings are positioned by their place in history; even installations, video art and performance are products of their time (I should know, having made some of this work myself).

Nothing lasts forever. I sometimes wonder if the gallery is in fact only a receptacle for events and personalities that have long since evaporated. What is left is merely a collection of what was once there, a shadow of art.

The people, the humanity are what count, not these dusty items on show. Objects are just a residue of process.

Imagine that instead of the artwork in front of you there is – nothing. Just a blank white wall.

What are you missing by this omission?

Concentrate on the feeling that is lost through the absence. Does it manifest as a yearning, a disappointment, a relief, a satisfaction?

Feel it through (the opposite of 'think it through'.)

Are you missing something?

Once you have accomplished this exercise, in your mind's eye, put it back on the wall and move on.

Art is a temporary object; all forms are unreal.

Remember this as you contemplate the gallery.

ARE YOU MISSING SOMETHING?

USE THE GALLERY AND ITS DOUBLE

The potential for magic is all around us.

On a visit to Tate Modern to look at the work of German photographer Otto Steinert, I saw an unmarked white door leading from the main gallery to a multi-faith and contemplation room, just off the beaten track.

When I went inside this space I felt that I was separate from the crowds, in a parallel dimension, out of time, floating agreeably in my own special universe.

I realised that the second room is always there, when we need it, as a shortcut to our creativity.

This area is the double of the main gallery; an interior territory that we can use to access ourselves. The art is merely a tool, a lever to propel us towards this new horizon.

The gallery and its double always exist.

(Thanks, Artaud.)

When you are looking at an artwork, step outside for a moment. Enter the 'double' white room, away from the crowds, where you can contemplate what you feel.

This manoeuvre might take just a few seconds. You are now in a transient space, an adjunct to reality, where you have a small distance from yourself.

In this moment of cognition, see if you can view the artwork with a new clarity.

(You can hold multiple views.)

YOU CAN HOLD MULTIPLE VIEWS.

CLIMB DOWN THE LADDER

Use any image to take you into this internal, 'double' space of the gallery – I visualise descending the rungs of a ladder, stepping down into the unconscious, into my deeper, primordial self.

Try it this way –

The Exercise

As you walk into the gallery space, imagine that things are changing.

Art is there to foster this transformation in you – and you are here to transform art. It doesn't necessarily offer you harmony; the results might be discordant or jarring.

Yet something is not the same.

I remember recently seeing David Hall's piece 'TV Interruptions' (1971) – short films that were originally conceived as television experiments. The installation at Tate Britain was shown on multiple TVs, jump-cutting between ambient noise and the volume of gushing water. The immediate impression was of cacophony. It was only on my second visit that I really got it – after much investment of time from myself.

The collision of sound and sight in 'TV Interruptions' pushed me into a relationship with my own unmediated core that was both intimidating and exciting.

Following my visit to David Hall's work, I thought 'the world is changing. I am changing and that's the reality'.

STEP DOWN INTO THE DEEPER, PRIMORDIAL SELF.

BECOME THE MAIN EVENT

If you are nervous of contemporary art, perhaps it's because of this: that the work doesn't necessarily offer the usual palette of colour or form.

It's not Manet, or Van Gogh, a classic that has endured, but it's possible to accept that fact and to look again at contemporary work as something new, worthy of investigation.

You have to persist, stepping down the ladder, like a performance of your own in which you are the main event.

The whole journey from home to station to bus to gallery ticket kiosk to shop might be viewed as an invisible performance in which you are a sort of 'artist' (I use this term loosely here).

Therefore, try any of the techniques already noted in this book before arriving at the gallery space –

- Spend 30 minutes.
- Totality.
- Write it down.
- Step into the work.
- Make a map.

All these methods can be adapted to the conditions of real life.

Look at yourself as a unique performance of one.

LOOK AT YOURSELF AS A UNIQUE PERFORMANCE OF ONE.

MIRROR YOURSELF

Another way of looking at a painting is to regard it as a mirror. You are seeing yourself within the work as you might be reflected in a polished surface; you are the form, the colour, the atmosphere, the content.

You are the painting.

If you focus on –

- Repetition
- Everyday
- Death
- Confusion
- Safety
- Conflict

then the work is that for you.

I recall in my teenage years I went to see an exhibition of Dada at The Hayward Gallery wearing a homemade badge on my lapel that said 'I Hate Dada'. Through this incontrovertible audacity I was trying to get in touch with the energy of Tristan Tzara, Louis Aragon and André Breton (my spiritual guides). I was attempting, in a primitive way, to be a reflection of art.

We regard the artist as a shaman, transforming base elements into new materials. We project this idea onto the creative artist. But, perhaps you can also do that?

Try mirroring yourself in the picture. What, in your everyday world, does this piece of art echo?

YOU
ARE THE
PAINTING.

CAVE PAINTING

Recently I was listening to George Lucas talk about his inspiration for the first 'Star Wars' film; he was drawing on Japanese filmmaker Akira Kurosawa for the depiction of the droids, using the most minor characters in the narrative to tell the story.

I found this very interesting – instead of beginning with grand visions of interplanetary warfare, he started in the mundane world of C-3PO and R2-D2: a junkyard, slavery, a decline.

It's a bit like what I'm asking you to do in this book – focus on the smallest elements.

Trust your own reactions.

Faced with the immensity of art, the big vistas, recognise that it's your part in the story that's important.

Simply regard art as sophisticated cave painting, making meaning of the everyday, directing your eye to a seeing of the world.

30,000 years later, it's still about that.

Often we equate size with grandeur of vision, of ambition. Instead shrink these large canvases back down to A4, to scratches on the wall of a cave, to pigment spat onto the rock.

What do they then become?

FOCUS ON THE SMALLEST ELEMENTS.

DESCRIBE IT IN ONE WORD

Use one word to describe what you see.

Is it –

- Bright?
- Conflicting?
- Serene?
- Uplifting?
- Dangerous?
- Blank?
- Confusing?
- Destructive?
- Exotic?
- Marginal?

Don't worry if the word is negative. The artwork doesn't always have to offer a positive outcome. It can provoke difficult feelings in you and still have some success.

Perhaps your tendency is to look for something that's beautiful and so, if you don't locate it immediately, you move on rapidly? If so, use the '30 minute technique' from the early part of this book to stay with your discomfort.

Look at it for longer. What do you really see? Explore all the parts of difficulty. After 30 minutes, what is the word you would use to describe it?

Has it changed?

THE ARTWORK DOESN'T ALWAYS HAVE TO OFFER A POSITIVE OUTCOME.

VISIT A SINGLE ITEM

Faced with the modern museum with all its distractions (boutiques, cafés, bookshops) and its volume of exhibits (collections, new exhibitions, archives), it's useful to visit one single item.

The Exercise

Choose something at random (it doesn't matter what it is). Look at it. Write your impressions, or draw them in your cheap notepad.

You will always find the same thing in it (you).

This might be a controversial idea. After all, wouldn't different pictures provoke different feelings in you? Isn't the idea that you would come back to the exact same reaction just absurd?

Yet, I find that the work of art is a funnel for what's happening at that moment inside of me. Different artworks will pick up on diverse parts of the emotional spectrum, but mostly it's all a version of me.

This is great – when I go to the art museum I am entering a giant amplifier of ME (M.E. My Exhibit).

Also, when you run this 'single item' exercise –

- Don't worry about setting an agenda.
- Don't worry about what I think.
- Don't worry about getting the exercise right.

Just look.

YOU ARE ENTERING A GIANT AMPLIFIER OF YOU.

START AT THE END AND WORK BACKWARDS

Another way of 'seeing' in the gallery is to evoke the opposite. Start at the end of the exhibition and retrace your steps.

This frequently provokes results because generally galleries don't like you to do this – there is a set route through which you should see the work: from early beginnings, via masterpieces to visionary endings.

Often I find that the museum won't let me enter the spaces in unconventional ways – this thwarts their modern sense of crowd control.

Therefore, I have to devise interesting strategies: I go in through the main door, speed through the exhibition and then slowly amble back in reverse mode.

I have to make a plan of 'how to see'.

This active methodology takes me out of my unconscious absorption of unquestioning process (what is given to me: the exhibition). It gives me a brief moment of cognition. Therefore, I step out of being a consumer of art and become active in generating my own reality.

I am aligned with my own responses.

'Start at the end and work backwards' is one action that encourages active seeing; it works because it physically alters your reading of the gallery space.

Become congruent with your feelings.

BECOME CONGRUENT WITH YOUR FEELINGS.

ZOOM OUT

Step out of yourself and zoom beyond the room as if you were looking at the whole gallery space from a distance.

I can give myself this idea of instant separation if I imagine that I am watching a programme about the object or artist on a foreign TV channel. In my mind's eye I reflect on others' cultural perspective on the material.

If it were a TV programme in –

- Japan
- Venezuela
- Egypt
- Greenland
- Taiwan

how might they report this item?

Zoom out further and imagine that you are looking from another planet. How might a visitor to Earth see this exhibition?

Do they witness –

- Difference?
- Spaciousness?
- Confusion?
- Elegance?

Another thought: if this visual item was made in the XIV Century, how would you regard it from the distance that time and hindsight now allows?

IMAGINE THAT YOU ARE LOOKING FROM ANOTHER PLANET.

ASK A CHILD'S OPINION

Ask someone who is more qualified than you – ask a child.

Often children are in the gallery and frequently they are responding to the work in instinctive ways, without the veneer of adult complicity (that we all add without even noticing it).

Sometimes I find this instinct of the child hard to tolerate: the actions of children in public spaces are loud, riotous, crude. Yet within that lack of subtlety there is a lot to recommend.

Often something cuts through that is uniquely perceptive, something that I haven't noticed before.

They might make an incisive suggestion that is totally apposite.

Once, at Tate Modern, I saw a mother and child looking at a copy of Louise Bourgeois' book 'The Puritan' in a glass vitrine. The child said 'I like this book', to which the mother replied 'It's just a load of rubbish. Pay no attention'.

In this instance, I preferred to follow the inclination of the youngster, rather than the mother's aggressive response. The child inside me was heartened by his sweet, enthusiastic reaction.

There is power in instinctive responses.

Support your own child by following a child's opinion, however bizarre or erratic that might appear.

SUPPORT YOUR OWN CHILD.

USE YOUR CURIOSITY

The child in you will encourage a certain presence, a curiosity that will help build a real connection with the art that you see. Not an ersatz response that anyone might have, but something that comes unmediated from you.

About –

- The body.
- Unrestrained joy.
- The boy or girl.
- Generosity.
- Doubt.

Or many other things.

(I can't say because I am not you.)

When you accommodate these responses, through presence and curiosity, then you really begin to use the gallery as a tool to fill yourself up with inspiration and aliveness.

The child is always central to this purpose.

Once, when I was showing my own large-scale 3-D digital projections in a gallery, I noticed that whilst the adults stood back, assessing the work, the children ran towards it, touching the walls, bathing themselves in the blue light. I often try to remember this when I am in the gallery.

I attempt to shed my ego, just for a moment, and dance in the work, as if it's all just play.

DANCE IN THE WORK, AS IF IT'S ALL JUST PLAY.

BE AUTHENTIC

Curiosity is the bridge that takes us from being a spectator of art to actively being a part of it, as a child might inhabit its own play.

Instead of only witnessing, putting art-historical language between us and the art object (in order to avoid it), we can step directly into the work.

I once went to an academic conference. During the debates, all the experts (myself included), made extensive records in their notepads.

It later occurred to me that this was an avoidance strategy on my part – if I presented complete documentation of the event, I would not expose myself and, therefore, could not be held personally culpable.

Instead, if I had chosen to stop writing and listened, I might have allowed myself to have an experience.

(With all the difficulty that it might engender.)

I could have used it as a tool to explore a more authentic self – not pushing away the embarrassment but pulling it towards me.

Therefore, be yourself. Don't always witness the work, or be a bystander, but have a real response that is true to you.

Make curiosity the conduit, the channel.

BE
YOURSELF.

STEP INSIDE THE IMAGE

One way of using yourself is to step into the image. Instead of looking at the picture, be it.

Try it this way –

The Exercise

Use 'I' to find the things that you can be within the picture. If it's Van Gogh's 'Sunflowers' (I choose this example as something that everyone recognises), say –

- I am sunny.
- I am flowers.
- I am a vase.
- I am a container.
- I am a petal.
- I am a seed.

Follow this journey for as long as you can, 1 minute minimum. Use any material that appears, however obscure it might seem.

Always use 'I'. This magic 'I' is often the element that allows you to connect with an authentic approach, rather than a remote attitude. Step into the image in this way, letting it enfold you. You can also apply this technique to the whole of your gallery experience.

- Be the seat that carries you on the train.
- Be the sunlight.
- Be the ticket that admits you to the gallery.

Be everything.

USE THE MAGIC 'I'.

LEAVE THE ROOM AND COME BACK

This movement, between self and artwork, totality and singularity, between the historical image and your individual reading of the picture, is a kind of exploratory process that allows you, the viewer, to test the possibilities.

It's experimental.

It doesn't use formulas. It avoids clichés and instead examines all the approaches, empirically running them against your own feelings.

Does any of what you see have meaning for you?

(You are the authority.)

You can try this approach in a physical way by moving in and out of the gallery space. Leave and come back.

What changes? This to and fro stops you from becoming blocked. You are less overwhelmed by the 'majesty' of the artist and so more willing to add your own voice.

The Exercise

Buy an annual member's pass so that you can visit the exhibition as often as you want. Therefore, you are not tied to routines like 'value for money' or 'I must persist'; even to worse scripts like 'it's not for me', 'I don't get it' or 'a child could do it'.

Floating free of these contemporary art clichés, you can find your own level.

DOES ANY
OF WHAT
YOU SEE
HAVE
MEANING
FOR YOU?

BE PREPARED TO EXIT

Generally, when we visit the art gallery, we tend to look at too much and so, overwhelmed by the material, find it difficult to have any clear view of what we are seeing.

The Exercise

Visit the gallery and look at one artwork, then leave.

What happens?

Hold it in your memory as you sit in the snack bar opposite the museum (it's called 'A Quick Bite') and reflect on what you have seen.

How does it abut against real life?

What is the journey between the gallery space and this prosaic environment? Trace the steps, the levels that you fall through on this return to the ordinary world.

Can you hold on to the heightened reality that art has given you?

As you think about these things, write down your ideas in your notepad, or on the disposable paper mat under your plate. Don't worry about what you write, just write.

Don't criticise yourself for not understanding art, or not having the originality that these great visual artists exhibit.

Just note your thoughts.

If you use your imagination, you are also an artist.

CAN YOU HOLD ON TO THE HEIGHTENED REALITY THAT ART HAS GIVEN YOU?

TAKE AWAY 90% OF THE IMAGE

This simple technique allows you to see in a new way.

In your mind's eye take away 90% of what you are looking at (it doesn't matter which 90% of the image you choose).

Please do not attempt any physical intervention into the artwork or try to remove anything – this is illegal and not the purpose of the exercise (see page 110).

Dispense with your ego. You are now left with 10% on which to focus your attention.

It might be –

- A corner.
- The entrance.
- A strip down the side.
- The title.
- A side of the canvas.
- The table legs.

The Exercise

Zoom in on the 10% that remains. Describe it in detail, or draw its content. What do you notice? Keep zooming until you find something previously unseen – a nail, a piece of varnish, a hair, a paint drip.

What does the varnish say to you? That the work is sticky, protected, shiny-coated?

Does it make you want to 'vanish'?

KEEP ZOOMING UNTIL YOU FIND SOMETHING PREVIOUSLY UNSEEN.

SHRINK IT

These 'zoomed' elements are the pieces that pierce the outside of the thing, activate your curiosity, allowing different and multiple readings of the artwork to take place, like a rhizome.

Another method is to shrink the piece.

Try it like this –

The Exercise

In your imagination reduce the size of any artwork to a postcard image that you can hold in your hand. In this reduced form, what does it say to you?

Any image expanded to giant size can have an impact, taking up the whole wall of a gallery. But what does it really say shrunk to a smaller format? Is it the same thing?

You can, of course, also apply this methodology to yourself and shrink your own form. If you imagine that your own grandiosity, volubility, pretension and aggrandisement are shrunk to the outline of an ordinary person, what happens? Stripped of any 'art-critic' aspirations, what do you really see?

During my whole time in the gallery, I try to observe this quality of ordinariness. I listen to what is around me, I watch others, I follow my instincts, I pay attention to the comings and goings of the space.

My aim is to be an ordinary person.

PAY ATTENTION TO THE COMINGS AND GOINGS OF THE SPACE.

ASK A STRANGER WHAT THEY THINK

As you make moves to leave the gallery, consider asking someone else what they think. I frequently do this to obtain another perspective on the work.

Observe the usual formalities of social etiquette – it's clear when people don't want to engage in a conversation. Usually I find, if approached with sensitivity, people are ready for dialogue.

Ask open questions –

- What do you see?
- Do you notice anything in particular?
- What draws your attention?
- Why pause here?

It's helpful to question people already in groups. This way it's less intrusive. Duos are good, or small clusters. That way you get multiple perspectives on what you are seeing.

Always say 'thank you' – it's polite.

Frequently people are in the space to explore other pathways, different strategies. So it's not so alien to them to be interrupted in their journey and asked for their views.

Tread softly but don't be afraid of offering your own opinion, especially if it's contrary to theirs.

All avenues open doors for everyone.

DON'T BE AFRAID OF OFFERING YOUR OWN OPINION.

YESTERDAY, TODAY, TOMORROW

Don't be critical of yourself if you can't 'interpret' what you see in front of you; there will always be the gallery tomorrow.

Art is a sounding board, an echo of where you are now; it will give you what you need right away, but there is always more. In the future, if you invest in yourself, you will 'interpret' more.

There is potential colour and philosophical intrigue; there is impact and sophisticated depth.

One way of doing this is to use colour.

The Exercise

Bring an item that has a colour to the gallery and hold it up at a distance from the piece, to add to or debate with the work on display.

This colour element can be fabric, a chocolate bar wrapper, the top of a fizzy soft drink bottle, an orange.

I frequently pick up these types of object on the way to the gallery, as a way of tuning in, making the street my intellectual mirror, in the manner of The Surrealists.

Suspend your colour item in thin air and see what it gives you. Can it offer you something of 'tomorrow' – the future of yourself or the artwork?

Where are you going to?

MAKE THE STREETS YOUR INTELLECTUAL MIRROR.

LEAVE THE GALLERY

At some point you will leave the gallery.

You will relinquish the safety of this protected space and venture into the unknown, the world beyond, what we call 'real' life.

How can you make a bridge between your art experience and your trajectory back home?

On this journey it's useful to protect yourself, to take some steps to guard against the volume of the outside.

These might appear silly or irrational, but there's nothing comical about protecting the soft inside of you against the hard surfaces of the world, against undue criticism or harsh knocks.

- Wear dark glasses.
- Take the shortest route.
- Put on your headphones.
- Make conscious steps.

The volume of the physical world might appear too bright or unduly noisy, so it's particularly useful to shield your eyes. Also, this stops other people, those who might criticise, looking in to you – the centre of which they might unconsciously want to diminish.

Don't linger but get home quickly. This transitional space is sometimes fraught with danger – don't hesitate.

Look to protect yourself.

LOOK TO PROTECT YOURSELF.

AFTERMATH

The vulnerable parts of you, the parts touched by art, can be quickly eroded, so it's useful to refer to your notepad frequently to remind yourself of the experiences that you have had.

These are real.

I say this because often you can doubt what happened to you. The drive of society is to perform, to achieve, to output. It's not towards self-actualisation, towards contemplation, towards individuation (Jung's term).

It's towards delivery – the nuts and bolts of an industrial paradigm.

Therefore, your soft processes must be protected.

It's not necessary to share your findings with anyone: even your family and close compatriots can be critical. Whilst not intending to hurt, they can still wound. So keep these events private, in a space marked 'do not open'.

Of course, ultimately, you might want to share your discoveries with other like-minded people, but be mindful of the need to protect yourself.

Many times I have been hurt by harsh words or cynical advice.

So my notepad has become the repository for private thoughts that I share with no one until they gain some further shape and can be distributed in the public domain.

IT'S NOT NECESSARY TO SHARE YOUR FINDINGS WITH ANYONE.

YOU, THE ARTIST

Your feelings can be channelled through your own creativity into something new.

After all, your writings on art and the sketches of objects that you have made in the gallery, as part of this book, are a vehicle for your own artistic practice.

This might not manifest straightaway, but over time, piece by piece, your sensibility will increase and can start to form something of your own, a portion that can be creative.

Why not you, the artist?

In this place, your vulnerability remains key. Your openness to the phenomena of the gallery and to the outside world is central (really, they are no different).

Support your own journey through these worlds with curiosity and calm.

The gallery is merely a filter for the creative process, but the possibilities are also all around you.

Look and keep looking.

Take any of the exercises in this book, directed towards art objects, and act them out beyond the gallery.

What if you looked at a drainpipe, or a bridge, or the rain, as the artwork?

WHY
NOT
YOU,
THE
ARTIST?

THE WOUND

My journey to art has been through the understanding of my own central wound.

The cut inside that is both pain and revelation.

In my equation, difficulty is the cure, the material that binds both together. Difficulty pushes me forward into the exactitude of the world.

Gnomic terms?

Obscurity? I don't think so.

In each of you, you have a wound that is the parallel of art, of art's vulnerability, and each time you witness artworks in all their depth and profundity, you will also feel this parallel pain in you.

Over time you can talk to this cut, make friends and believe in its power – it can protect you. You can choose how to work with it. You can select which parts of it to internalise and which to leave behind.

(But perhaps this is a different book?)

As you move from the gallery into real life, all sorts of things grapple for your attention, your love.

In the art space you can remain for a few moments, seconds, outside these demands.

Pure.

YOU HAVE A WOUND THAT IS THE PARALLEL OF ART'S VULNERABILITY.

ENDINGS

As I come to the end of this book, I feel the difficulty of leaving behind me the subject of the gallery.

Immersion in art allows us for a few moments to avoid the pressing concerns of real life. Even if the work is about these issues, it encourage a suspension in something else.

The fantasy?

Therefore, when we leave the art gallery behind, we step out into the void. The artworks have protected us for a while; they nurture our sensibility. Sometimes it's a great shock when the lights go out and we have to go home.

As I leave this text behind, I remember that the journey through art is with feelings. Everything that I see with my eyes, everything that I regard, is me. All the artworks, although made by other people, are versions of me. They point towards parts of myself and help my onward journey towards consciousness.

I end with 'I'.

'I feel', 'I understand', 'I believe'.

I
Me
Myself
Mine

I walk out of the space, enlivened by its perspicacity and sensitivity.

THE JOURNEY THROUGH ART IS WITH FEELINGS.

MICHAEL ATAVAR

Michael Atavar is an artist and a creative consultant with a practice that mixes creativity, business, art and psychology.

He works with individuals and businesses, helping to solve professional problems, using creativity as a key.

www.creativepractice.com

ACKNOWLEDGEMENTS

The first draft of the book was written in January 2016 on Causse Méjean: thanks to Pascale Darchy and Neil Robinson for their hospitality.

Thank you to Roelof Bakker, Kelly Coe, Martin Crawley, Miles Hanson, Jonathan Kemp, Joseph Kendra, Jackie de Lima, Wiebke Pausch, Richard Scarborough, Steven Whinnery.

The Latin quote is my own inversion of Marcus Cicero.

Thanks to Sgnuj.

Tate name and logo are reproduced by permission of the Tate Trustees.

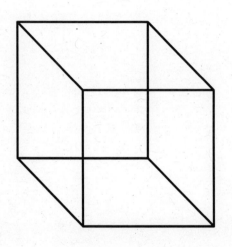

EPILOGUE — USING MENTAL TECHNIQUES

This is a book of mental techniques.

It does not encourage any physical engagement with publicly displayed art.

Do not touch, interfere with, remove from the space or access any of the artworks that you are looking at, unless there is an express written or verbal invitation from the gallery on behalf of the artists.

In situations where the artwork invites contributions from the public, please go ahead, but observe the usual limits that operate in these shared environments.

Otherwise, look, see, feel but don't touch.

Stay behind the cordoned-off areas.

In the book, when I invoke your personal responses, I mean that they are true for you; I don't mean to suggest that your version of reality is more real than someone else's or gives you a licence to act on that belief.

Use modesty as your ultimate guide; respect the boundaries of the space.

If you want to act, if you feel compelled, make your own art – take the inspiration of the gallery away with you and create artwork. If you feel drawn to interventions, consider a career as a performance artist.

Only test your limits within the safe space of your own creativity.